MW00712775

THIS BOOK BELONGS TO

_____

START DATE

_____

SHE READS TRUTH

@SHEREADSTRUTH

Download the
She Reads Truth app,
available for iOS
and Android.

Subscribe to the
She Reads Truth podcast

SHEREADSTRUTH.COM

EXECUTIVE

FOUNDER/CHIEF EXECUTIVE OFFICER
Raechel Myers

CO-FOUNDER/CHIEF CONTENT OFFICER
Amanda Bible Williams

CHIEF OPERATING OFFICER
Ryan Myers

EXECUTIVE ASSISTANT
Catherine Cromer

EDITORIAL

CONTENT DIRECTOR
John Greco, MDiv

MANAGING EDITOR
Jessica Lamb

CONTENT EDITOR
Kara Gause

ASSOCIATE EDITORS
Bailey Gillespie
Ellen Taylor

CREATIVE

CREATIVE DIRECTOR
Jeremy Mitchell

LEAD DESIGNER
Kelsea Allen

DESIGNERS
Abbey Benson
Davis DeLisi

MARKETING

MARKETING DIRECTOR
Hannah Warren

MARKETING MANAGER
Katie Matuska

SOCIAL MEDIA MANAGER
Ansley Rushing

PARTNERSHIP SPECIALIST
Kamiren Passavanti

COMMUNITY SUPPORT SPECIALIST
Margot Williams

SHIPPING & LOGISTICS

LOGISTICS MANAGER
Lauren Gloyne

SHIPPING MANAGER
Sydney Bess

CUSTOMER SUPPORT SPECIALIST
Katy McKnight

FULFILLMENT SPECIALISTS
Sam Campos
Julia Rogers

SUBSCRIPTION INQUIRIES
orders@shereadstruth.com

CONTRIBUTORS

PHOTOGRAPHER
Heather Burris (Cover, 20, 28, 36, 42,
52, 58, 64, 70, 76)

SHE READS TRUTH™

© 2019 by She Reads Truth, LLC

All rights reserved.

All photography used by permission.

ISBN 978-1-949526-78-3

1 2 3 4 5 6 7 8 9 10

Research support provided by Logos Bible Software™. Learn more at logos.com.

Though the dates in this book have been carefully researched, scholars disagree on the dating of many biblical events.

This book was printed offset in Nashville, Tennessee, on 70# Lynx Opaque. Cover is 100# Cougar Opaque with a soft touch lamination.

1, 2 & 3 JOHN

THIS IS LOVE

"Little children,
love one another."

Jessica

Jessica Lamb
MANAGING EDITOR

One of my favorite stories from the early Church fathers is about the teaching ministry of the apostle John, who penned these three letters, as well as the Gospel of John and the book of Revelation.

The story holds that John lived in Ephesus until he was very, very old. Despite his advanced age, he still made it a priority to teach the brothers and sisters in Ephesus at church gatherings, even if it meant his disciples had to carry him there and back. And of course they did, because imagine all the things John could share: John, called to leave his fishing nets and follow Jesus (Mt 4:21–22). John, who walked with Jesus during His earthly ministry, listening to His teaching every day and witnessing His miracles. John, one of only three disciples to see Jesus in His transfigured glory and the only one of the Twelve who stayed near Jesus at the cross (Mk 9:2–10; Jn 19:25–27). He's the disciple who outran Peter in his eagerness to see the empty tomb, and he ate fish on the beach with the risen Christ (Jn 20:1–9; 21:1–14).

But, according to tradition, John did not teach on these things. Instead, he would say the same thing at every gathering, every single time: "Little children, love one another." Finally, those in attendance asked him why he didn't vary from this script. John replied, "Because it is the Lord's commandment to us, and if it alone is kept, it is sufficient."

Now, this story is more legend than proven history. But as you'll notice when you read these letters, John returns to the importance of love repeatedly—over fifty times in 133 verses! In John 13:34–35, he records Jesus giving His disciples this command: "Love one another. Just as I have loved you, you are also to love one another. By this everyone will know that you are my disciples." The letters of 1, 2, and 3 John make it clear that this command from Christ is not optional. It is essential to how we live as His disciples.

We've included several extras in this Study Book to help you dig deeper into the text. The "Gospel Connections" resource on page 14 shows how these letters connect to the themes in John's Gospel. We've also included an exploration of some of the Hebrew and Greek terms translated as "love" in our English Bibles (p. 50), a look at the gospel assurances detailed in John's letters (p. 74), and a flow chart answering some common objections we have to loving one another.

Whenever these letters are read today, John's message is repeated yet again: "Little children, love one another." Let it be so!

DESIGN ON PURPOSE

At She Reads Truth, we believe in pairing the inherently beautiful Word of God with the aesthetic beauty it deserves. Each of our resources is thoughtfully and artfully designed to highlight the beauty, goodness, and truth of Scripture in a way that reflects the themes of each curated reading plan.

We chose to use black and white photography throughout this book to highlight the contrasting imagery within the text. Light guides the eye through these photos, an allusion to the gospel-centered love that should guide our lives in Christ.

The high contrast letterforms of Didot elevate the tension and conflict that John describes—light and darkness, love and hate, sin and forgiveness, truth and falsehood. Also soft and elegant, these letterforms represent the call to biblical love that echoes throughout these letters.

She Reads Truth is a community of women dedicated to reading the Word of God every day.

The Bible is living and active, breathed out by God, and we confidently hold it higher than anything we can do or say. This book focuses primarily on Scripture, with bonus resources to facilitate deeper engagement with God's Word.

SCRIPTURE READING

Designed for a Monday start, this Study Book presents the books of 1, 2, and 3 John in daily readings, with supplemental passages for additional context.

Throughout this reading plan are examples of themes that connect the Gospel of John to the letters of John. Text from the Gospel of John will be included alongside the relevant 1, 2, or 3 John reading.

JOURNALING SPACE

Each weekday includes space for reflection and a prompt for prayer.

GRACE DAY

Use Saturdays to pray, rest, and reflect on what you've read.

WEEKLY TRUTH

Sundays are set aside for weekly Scripture memorization.

Find the corresponding memory cards in the back of this book.

EXTRAS

This book features additional tools to help you gain a deeper understanding of the text.

For added community and conversation, join us in the **1, 2 & 3 John** reading plan on the She Reads Truth app or at SheReadsTruth.com—where women from Chattanooga to China will be reading along with you!

1, 2 & 3 John

2 Weeks

PLAN OVERVIEW

"This is the command us you have heard it from the beginning: that you walk in love." In his three letters to early believers, John encourages Christians to honor God's commands by avoiding destructive patterns and beliefs. John's exhortation is a call to action for all of us—to embody Christ's love and contribute to the flourishing of the Church. As we grow in our knowledge of God, we learn how to extend the same love and forgiveness to a broken world that God first showed us.

TABLE OF
CONTENTS

WEEK ONE

1

WEEK TWO

2

SHE READS
1, 2 & 3 JOHN

On the Timeline

Second-century sources reported that around AD 70, the year the Romans destroyed Jerusalem and the temple, John left Jerusalem, where he was a church leader, and relocated to Ephesus. He continued his pastoral work in that region and lived until nearly AD 100. Ephesus is likely the place where John wrote the three New Testament letters that bear his name. They could have been composed at any time in the last quarter of the first century.

A Little Background

Ancient manuscripts are unanimous in naming John as the author of 1 John. The son of Zebedee, John was "the disciple Jesus loved" (Jn 21:20), who also authored the Fourth Gospel. "The elder" (2Jn 1) is a title the apostle John applied to himself late in life. (The apostle Peter referred to himself the same way in 1 Peter 5:1.) No one other than the apostle John was ever suggested by the early Church as the writer of 1 John and, since there are so many similarities between 1, 2, and 3 John, it is generally accepted that John wrote all three letters.

GOSPEL CONNECTIONS

Most Bible scholars believe that the letters we know today as 1, 2, and 3 John were penned by the author of the Gospel of John, traditionally thought to be John, the son of Zebedee and a disciple of Jesus. One support for this theory is the number of thematic connections between the works. These parallels point not only to a common author, but also to the unchanging nature of the gospel message, "the message we have heard from him and declare to you" (1Jn 1:5).

Listed here, and noted in margins throughout the book, are examples that connect the Gospel of John to the letters of John.

This is the message we have heard from him and declare to you: God is light, and there is absolutely no darkness in him. If we say, "We have fellowship with him," and yet we walk in darkness, we are lying and are not practicing the truth. If we walk in the light as he himself is in the light, we have fellowship with one another, and the blood of Jesus his Son cleanses us from all sin.

1JN 1:5–7

Being in the Light

JN 8:12

Jesus spoke to them again: "I am the light of the world. Anyone who follows me will never walk in the darkness but will have the light of life."

If you know that he is righteous, you know this as well: Everyone who does what is right has been born of him.

1JN 2:29

Being Born of God

JN 1:12–13

But to all who did receive him, he gave them the right to be children of God, to those who believe in his name, who were born, not of natural descent, or of the will of the flesh, or of the will of man, but of God.

Do not be surprised, brothers and sisters, if the world hates you.

1JN 3:13

We know that we have passed from death to life because we love our brothers and sisters. The one who does not love remains in death.

1JN 3:14

This is how we have come to know love: He laid down his life for us.

1JN 3:16

Being Hated by the World

Having Passed from Death to Life

Knowing the Greatest Love

JN 15:18–19

JN 5:24

JN 15:12–13

"If the world hates you, understand that it hated me before it hated you. If you were of the world, the world would love you as its own. However, because you are not of the world, but I have chosen you out of it, the world hates you."

"Truly I tell you, anyone who hears my word and believes him who sent me has eternal life and will not come under judgment but has passed from death to life."

"This is my command: Love one another as I have loved you. No one has greater love than this: to lay down his life for his friends."

The one who keeps his commands remains in him, and he in him. And the way we know that he remains in us is from the Spirit he has given us.

1 JN 3:24

God's love was revealed among us in this way: God sent his one and only Son into the world so that we might live through him.

1 JN 4:9

So now I ask you, dear lady—not as if I were writing you a new command, but one we have had from the beginning—that we love one another.

2 JN 5

Remaining in Christ

*Seeing God's Love
Revealed in the Son*

Loving One Another

JN 15:4

JN 3:16

JN 13:34

"Remain in me, and I in you. Just as a branch is unable to produce fruit by itself unless it remains on the vine, neither can you unless you remain in me."

"For God loved the world in this way: He gave his one and only Son, so that everyone who believes in him will not perish but have eternal life."

"I give you a new command: Love one another. Just as I have loved you, you are also to love one another."

Many deceivers have gone out into the world; they do not confess the coming of Jesus Christ in the flesh. This is the deceiver and the antichrist.

2JN 7

Though I have many things to write to you, I don't want to use paper and ink. Instead, I hope to come to you and talk face to face so that our joy may be complete.

2JN 12

For I was very glad when fellow believers came and testified to your fidelity to the truth—how you are walking in truth.

3JN 3

Believing the Son of God Came in the Flesh

Having Joy Made Complete

Knowing the Truth

JN 1:14

JN 15:11

JN 18:37

The Word became flesh and dwelt among us. We observed his glory, the glory as the one and only Son from the Father, full of grace and truth.

"I have told you these things so that my joy may be in you and your joy may be complete."

"You are a king then?" Pilate asked.

"You say that I'm a king," Jesus replied. "I was born for this, and I have come into the world for this: to testify to the truth. Everyone who is of the truth listens to my voice."

*IF WE CONFESS OUR
SINS, HE IS FAITHFUL
AND RIGHTEOUS
TO FORGIVE US
OUR SINS AND TO
CLEANSE US FROM ALL
UNRIGHTEOUSNESS.*

Message & Purpose

First John was written to help early Christians confirm their faith and avoid destructive beliefs and behaviors.

John gives four purpose statements:

1 We are writing these things so that our joy may be complete. **1JN 1:4**

2 My little children, I am writing you these things so that you may not sin. **1JN 2:1**

3 I have written these things to you concerning those who are trying to deceive you. **1JN 2:26**

4 I have written these things to you who believe in the name of the Son of God so that you may know that you have eternal life. **1JN 5:13**

The last purpose statement governs the other three and brings them together in a unifying theme.

Give Thanks for the Book of 1 John

First John maps out the three main components of the saving knowledge of God: faith in Jesus Christ, obedient response to God's commands, and love for God and others from the heart. This epistle shows how Jesus expects His followers to honor Him in practical church life and wherever God calls His people to go and serve.

FELLOWSHIP WITH GOD

1 John 1; Numbers 14:18–19; Matthew 28:18–20; John 1:1–5

1 John 1

PROLOGUE: OUR DECLARATION

[1] What was from the beginning, what we have heard, what we have seen with our eyes, what we have observed and have touched with our hands, concerning the word of life— [2] that life was revealed, and we have seen it and we testify and declare to you the eternal life that was with the Father and was revealed to us— [3] what we have seen and heard we also declare to you, so that you may also have fellowship with us; and indeed our fellowship is with the Father and with his Son Jesus Christ. [4] We are writing these things so that our joy may be complete.

FELLOWSHIP WITH GOD

GOSPEL CONNECTION

Jesus spoke to them again: "I am the light of the world. Anyone who follows me will never walk in the darkness but will have the light of life."

JN 8:12

[5] This is the message we have heard from him and declare to you: God is light, and there is absolutely no darkness in him. [6] If we say, "We have fellowship with him," and yet we walk in darkness, we are lying and are not practicing the truth. [7] If we walk in the light as he himself is in the light, we have fellowship with one another, and the blood of Jesus his Son cleanses us from all sin. [8] If we say, "We have no sin," we are deceiving ourselves, and the truth is not in us. [9] If we confess our sins, he is faithful and righteous to forgive us our sins and to cleanse us from all unrighteousness. [10] If we say, "We have not sinned," we make him a liar, and his word is not in us.

Numbers 14:18–19

[18] "The LORD is slow to anger and abounding in faithful love, forgiving iniquity and rebellion. But he will not leave the guilty unpunished, bringing the consequences of the fathers' iniquity on the children to the third and fourth generation. [19] Please pardon the iniquity of this people, in keeping with the greatness of your faithful love, just as you have forgiven them from Egypt until now."

Matthew 28:18–20

[18] Jesus came near and said to them, "All authority has been given to me in heaven and on earth. [19] Go, therefore, and make disciples of all nations, baptizing them in the name of the Father and of the Son and of the Holy Spirit, [20] teaching them to observe everything I have commanded you. And remember, I am with you always, to the end of the age."

PROLOGUE

[1] In the beginning was the Word, and the Word was with God, and the Word was God. [2] He was with God in the beginning. [3] All things were created through him, and apart from him not one thing was created that has been created. [4] In him was life, and that life was the light of men. [5] That light shines in the darkness, and yet the darkness did not overcome it.

*If we walk in the light as he himself is
in the light, we have fellowship with
one another, and the blood of Jesus his
Son cleanses us from all sin.*

1 JOHN 1:7

KEEPING GOD'S COMMANDS

1 John 2:1–14; Matthew 11:25–30; Ephesians 6:10–20; 1 Timothy 2:5–6

1 John 2:1–14

¹ My little children, I am writing you these things so that you may not sin. But if anyone does sin, we have an advocate with the Father—Jesus Christ the righteous one. ² He himself is the atoning sacrifice for our sins, and not only for ours, but also for those of the whole world.

GOD'S COMMANDS

³ This is how we know that we know him: if we keep his commands. ⁴ The one who says, "I have come to know him," and yet doesn't keep his commands, is a liar, and the truth is not in him. ⁵ But whoever keeps his word, truly in him the love of God is made complete. This is how we know we are in him: ⁶ The one who says he remains in him should walk just as he walked.

⁷ Dear friends, I am not writing you a new command but an old command that you have had from the beginning. The old command is the word you have heard. ⁸ Yet I am writing you a new command, which is true in him and in you, because the darkness is passing away and the true light is already shining. ⁹ The one who says he is in the light but hates his brother or sister is in the darkness until now. ¹⁰ The one who loves his brother or sister remains in the light, and there is no cause for stumbling in him. ¹¹ But the one who hates his brother or sister is in the darkness, walks in the darkness, and doesn't know where he's going, because the darkness has blinded his eyes.

[12] I am writing to you, little children,
since your sins have been forgiven
on account of his name.
[13] I am writing to you, fathers,
because you have come to know
the one who is from the beginning.
I am writing to you, young men,
because you have conquered the evil one.
[14] I have written to you, children,
because you have come to know the Father.
I have written to you, fathers,
because you have come to know
the one who is from the beginning.
I have written to you, young men,
because you are strong,
God's word remains in you,
and you have conquered the evil one.

> BUT WHOEVER
> KEEPS HIS
> WORD, TRULY
> IN HIM THE
> LOVE OF
> GOD IS MADE
> COMPLETE.
>
> 1 JOHN 2:5

Matthew 11:25–30

THE SON GIVES KNOWLEDGE AND REST

[25] At that time Jesus said, "I praise you, Father, Lord of heaven and earth, because you have hidden these things from the wise and intelligent and revealed them to infants. [26] Yes, Father, because this was your good pleasure. [27] All things have been entrusted to me by my Father. No one knows the Son except the Father, and no one knows the Father except the Son and anyone to whom the Son desires to reveal him.

[28] "Come to me, all of you who are weary and burdened, and I will give you rest. [29] Take up my yoke and learn from me, because I am lowly and humble in heart, and you will find rest for your souls. [30] For my yoke is easy and my burden is light."

Ephesians 6:10–20

CHRISTIAN WARFARE

[10] Finally, be strengthened by the Lord and by his vast strength. [11] Put on the full armor of God so that you can stand against the schemes of the devil. [12] For our struggle is not against flesh and blood, but against the rulers, against the authorities, against the cosmic powers of this darkness, against evil, spiritual forces in the heavens. [13] For this reason take up the full armor of God, so that you may

be able to resist in the evil day, and having prepared everything, to take your stand. [14] Stand, therefore, with truth like a belt around your waist, righteousness like armor on your chest, [15] and your feet sandaled with readiness for the gospel of peace. [16] In every situation take up the shield of faith with which you can extinguish all the flaming arrows of the evil one. [17] Take the helmet of salvation and the sword of the Spirit—which is the word of God. [18] Pray at all times in the Spirit with every prayer and request, and stay alert with all perseverance and intercession for all the saints. [19] Pray also for me, that the message may be given to me when I open my mouth to make known with boldness the mystery of the gospel. [20] For this I am an ambassador in chains. Pray that I might be bold enough to speak about it as I should.

1 Timothy 2:5–6

[5] For there is one God and one mediator between God and humanity, the man Christ Jesus, [6] who gave himself as a ransom for all, a testimony at the proper time.

*This is how we know that we know
him: if we keep his commands.*

1 JOHN 2:3

_____

_____

_____

_____

_____

_____

_____

_____

_____

_____

_____

_____

_____

_____

REMAINING IN GOD

1 John 2:15–27; Isaiah 61:1–4; James 4:4–7

1 John 2:15–27

A WARNING ABOUT THE WORLD

[15] Do not love the world or the things in the world. If anyone loves the world, the love of the Father is not in him. [16] For everything in the world—the lust of the flesh, the lust of the eyes, and the pride in one's possessions—is not from the Father, but is from the world. [17] And the world with its lust is passing away, but the one who does the will of God remains forever.

THE LAST HOUR

[18] Children, it is the last hour. And as you have heard that antichrist is coming, even now many antichrists have come. By this we know that it is the last hour. [19] They went out from us, but they did not belong to us; for if they had belonged to us, they would have remained with us. However, they went out so that it might be made clear that none of them belongs to us.

[20] But you have an anointing from the Holy One, and all of you know the truth. [21] I have not written to you because you don't know the truth, but because you do know it, and because no lie comes from the truth. [22] Who is the liar, if not the one who denies that Jesus is the Christ? This one is the antichrist: the one who denies the Father and the Son. [23] No one who denies the Son has the Father; he who confesses the Son has the Father as well.

REMAINING WITH GOD

[24] What you have heard from the beginning is to remain in you. If what you have heard from the beginning remains in you, then you will remain in the Son and in the Father. [25] And this is the promise that he himself made to us: eternal life.

[26] I have written these things to you concerning those who are trying to deceive you. [27] As for you, the anointing you received from him remains in you, and you don't need anyone to teach you. Instead, his anointing teaches you about all things and is true and is not a lie; just as it has taught you, remain in him.

WHAT YOU HAVE HEARD FROM THE BEGINNING IS TO REMAIN IN YOU.

1 JOHN 2:24

Isaiah 61:1–4

MESSIAH'S JUBILEE

¹ The Spirit of the Lord God is on me,
because the Lord has anointed me
to bring good news to the poor.
He has sent me to heal the brokenhearted,
to proclaim liberty to the captives
and freedom to the prisoners;
² to proclaim the year of the Lord's favor,
and the day of our God's vengeance;
to comfort all who mourn,
³ to provide for those who mourn in Zion;
to give them a crown of beauty instead of ashes,
festive oil instead of mourning,
and splendid clothes instead of despair.
And they will be called righteous trees,
planted by the Lord
to glorify him.
⁴ They will rebuild the ancient ruins;
they will restore the former devastations;
they will renew the ruined cities,
the devastations of many generations.

James 4:4–7

⁴ You adulterous people! Don't you know that friendship with the world is hostility toward God? So whoever wants to be the friend of the world becomes the enemy of God. ⁵ Or do you think it's without reason that the Scripture says: The spirit he made to dwell in us envies intensely?

⁶ But he gives greater grace. Therefore he says:

God resists the proud,
but gives grace to the humble.

⁷ Therefore, submit to God. Resist the devil, and he will flee from you.

*If what you have heard from the
beginning remains in you, then you will
remain in the Son and in the Father.*

1 JOHN 2:24

WE ARE GOD'S CHILDREN

1 John 2:28–29; 1 John 3:1–10; John 3:1–15; James 1:19–27

GOSPEL CONNECTION

But to all who did receive him, he gave them the right to be children of God, to those who believe in his name, who were born, not of natural descent, or of the will of the flesh, or of the will of man, but of God.

JN 1:12–13

1 John 2:28–29

GOD'S CHILDREN

[28] So now, little children, remain in him so that when he appears we may have confidence and not be ashamed before him at his coming. [29] **If you know that he is righteous, you know this as well: Everyone who does what is right has been born of him.**

1 John 3:1–10

[1] See what great love the Father has given us that we should be called God's children—and we are! The reason the world does not know us is that it didn't know him. [2] Dear friends, we are God's children now, and what we will be has not yet been revealed. We know that when he appears, we will be like him because we will see him as he is. [3] And everyone who has this hope in him purifies himself just as he is pure.

[4] Everyone who commits sin practices lawlessness; and sin is lawlessness. [5] You know that he was revealed so that he might take away sins, and there is no sin in him. [6] Everyone who remains in him does not sin; everyone who sins has not seen him or known him.

⁷ Children, let no one deceive you. The one who does what is right is righteous, just as he is righteous. ⁸ The one who commits sin is of the devil, for the devil has sinned the beginning. The Son of God was revealed for this purpose: to destroy the devil's works. ⁹ Everyone who has been born of God does not sin, because his seed remains in him; he is not able to sin, because he has been born of God. ¹⁰ This is how God's children and the devil's children become obvious. Whoever does not do what is right is not of God, especially the one who does not love his brother or sister.

John 3:1–15

JESUS AND NICODEMUS

¹ There was a man from the Pharisees named Nicodemus, a ruler of the Jews. ² This man came to him at night and said, "Rabbi, we know that you are a teacher who has come from God, for no one could perform these signs you do unless God were with him."

³ Jesus replied, "Truly I tell you, unless someone is born again, he cannot see the kingdom of God."

⁴ "How can anyone be born when he is old?" Nicodemus asked him. "Can he enter his mother's womb a second time and be born?"

⁵ Jesus answered, "Truly I tell you, unless someone is born of water and the Spirit, he cannot enter the kingdom of God. ⁶ Whatever is born of the flesh is flesh, and whatever is born of the Spirit is spirit. ⁷ Do not be amazed that I told you that you must be born again. ⁸ The wind blows where it pleases, and you hear its sound, but you don't know where it comes from or where it is going. So it is with everyone born of the Spirit."

⁹ "How can these things be?" asked Nicodemus.

¹⁰ "Are you a teacher of Israel and don't know these things?" Jesus replied. ¹¹ "Truly I tell you, we speak what we know and we testify to what we have seen, but you do not accept our testimony. ¹² If I have told you about earthly things and you don't believe, how will you believe if I tell you about heavenly things? ¹³ No one has ascended into heaven except the one who descended from heaven —the Son of Man.

¹⁴ "Just as Moses lifted up the snake in the wilderness, so the Son of Man must be lifted up, ¹⁵ so that everyone who believes in him may have eternal life."

HEARING AND DOING THE WORD

[19] My dear brothers and sisters, understand this: Everyone should be quick to listen, slow to speak, and slow to anger, [20] for human anger does not accomplish God's righteousness. [21] Therefore, ridding yourselves of all moral filth and the evil that is so prevalent, humbly receive the implanted word, which is able to save your souls.

[22] But be doers of the word and not hearers only, deceiving yourselves. [23] Because if anyone is a hearer of the word and not a doer, he is like someone looking at his own face in a mirror. [24] For he looks at himself, goes away, and immediately forgets what kind of person he was. [25] But the one who looks intently into the perfect law of freedom and perseveres in it, and is not a forgetful hearer but a doer who works—this person will be blessed in what he does.

[26] If anyone thinks he is religious without controlling his tongue, his religion is useless and he deceives himself. [27] Pure and undefiled religion before God the Father is this: to look after orphans and widows in their distress and to keep oneself unstained from the world.

USE THIS VERSE FROM
YOUR DAILY READING AS
A PROMPT FOR PRAYER.

*Dear friends, we are God's children now,
and what we will be has not yet been
revealed. We know that when he appears,
we will be like him because we will see
him as he is.*

1 JOHN 3:2

_____

_____

_____

_____

_____

_____

_____

_____

_____

_____

_____

_____

LOVE IN ACTION

1 John 3:11–24; Deuteronomy 15:7–11; John 16:7–14; Romans 12:9

LOVE IN ACTION

[11] For this is the message you have heard from the beginning: We should love one another, [12] unlike Cain, who was of the evil one and murdered his brother. And why did he murder him? Because his deeds were evil, and his brother's were righteous.

[13] Do not be surprised, brothers and sisters, if the world hates you. [14] We know that we have passed from death to life because we love our brothers and sisters. The one who does not love remains in death. [15] Everyone who hates his brother or sister is a murderer, and you know that no murderer has eternal life residing in him. [16] This is how we have come to know love: He laid down his life for us. We should also lay down our lives for our brothers and sisters. [17] If anyone has this world's goods and sees a fellow believer in need but withholds compassion from him—how does God's love reside in him? [18] Little children, let us not love in word or speech, but in action and in truth.

[19] This is how we will know that we belong to the truth and will reassure our hearts before him [20] whenever our hearts condemn us; for God is greater than our hearts, and he knows all things.

[21] Dear friends, if our hearts don't condemn us, we have confidence before God [22] and receive whatever we ask from him because we keep his commands and do what is pleasing in his sight. [23] Now this is his command: that we believe in the name of his Son Jesus Christ, and love one another as he commanded us. [24] The one who keeps his commands remains in him, and he in him. And the way we know that he remains in us is from the Spirit he has given us.

GOSPEL CONNECTION

"If the world hates you, understand that it hated me before it hated you. If you were of the world, the world would love you as its own. However, because you are not of the world, but I have chosen you out of it, the world hates you."

JN 15:18–19

GOSPEL CONNECTION

"This is my command: Love one another as I have loved you. No one has greater love than this: to lay down his life for his friends."

JN 15:12–13

GOSPEL CONNECTION

"Truly I tell you, anyone who hears my word and believes him who sent me has eternal life and will not come under judgment but has passed from death to life."

JN 5:24

GOSPEL CONNECTION

"Remain in me, and I in you. Just as a branch is unable to produce fruit by itself unless it remains on the vine, neither can you unless you remain in me."

JN 15:4

Deuteronomy 15:7–11

LENDING TO THE POOR

[7] "If there is a poor person among you, one of your brothers within any of your city gates in the land the LORD your God is giving you, do not be hardhearted or tightfisted toward your poor brother. [8] Instead, you are to open your hand to him and freely loan him enough for whatever need he has. [9] Be careful that there isn't this wicked thought in your heart, 'The seventh year, the year of canceling debts, is near,' and you are stingy toward your poor brother and give him nothing. He will cry out to the LORD against you, and you will be guilty. [10] Give to him, and don't have a stingy heart when you give, and because of this the LORD your God will bless you in all your work and in everything you do. [11] For there will never cease to be poor people in the land; that is why I am commanding you, 'Open your hand willingly to your poor and needy brother in your land.'"

John 16:7–14

[7] "Nevertheless, I am telling you the truth. It is for your benefit that I go away, because if I don't go away the Counselor will not come to you. If I go, I will send him to you. [8] When he comes, he will convict the world about sin, righteousness, and judgment: [9] About sin, because they do not believe in me; [10] about righteousness, because I am going to the Father and you will no longer see me; [11] and about judgment, because the ruler of this world has been judged.

[12] "I still have many things to tell you, but you can't bear them now. [13] When the Spirit of truth comes, he will guide you into all the truth. For he will not speak on his own, but he will speak whatever he hears. He will also declare to you what is to come. [14] He will glorify me, because he will take from what is mine and declare it to you."

Romans 12:9

Let love be without hypocrisy. Detest evil; cling to what is good.

USE THIS VERSE FROM
YOUR DAILY READING AS
A PROMPT FOR PRAYER.

*This is how we have come to know
love: He laid down his life for us. We
should also lay down our lives for our
brothers and sisters.*

1 JOHN 3:16

PREP TIME	RISE TIME	BAKE TIME
10 minutes	26 hours	40 minutes

NO-KNEAD BREAD

Ingredients

3 cups ull-purpose or gluten-free flour

1 tablespoon fresh rosemary, chopped

1 teaspoon garlic powder

1¼ teaspoons salt

1 teaspoon black pepper

½ teaspoon active yeast

1½ cups water, room temperature

Directions

Whisk together flour, rosemary, garlic powder, salt, pepper, and yeast in a large bowl.

Using a wooden spoon, add water then mix until combined into a sticky dough.

Cover bowl tighty with lid or plastic wrap and let sit at room temperature for 24 hours.

Lightly oil a cast iron skillet or round pan. Pour dough from bowl into skillet. Cover with a towel and let sit for 2 more hours at room temperature, until the dough has doubled to fill the pan.

Preheat oven to 425°F. Bake until golden brown, about 40 minutes.

Double this recipe and deliver the second loaf to a friend or neighbor!

GRACE DAY

6

*Use today to pray, rest, and
reflect on this week's reading,
giving thanks for the grace
that is ours in Christ.*

NOW THIS IS HIS
COMMAND: THAT WE
BELIEVE IN THE NAME OF
HIS SON JESUS CHRIST,
AND LOVE ONE ANOTHER
AS HE COMMANDED US.

1 JOHN 3:23

WEEKLY TRUTH

7

Scripture is God-breathed and true. When we memorize it, we carry the gospel with us wherever we go.

This week we will memorize the key verse for 1 John, a declaration of God's love and faithfulness.

*IF WE CONFESS OUR
SINS, HE IS FAITHFUL
AND RIGHTEOUS
TO FORGIVE US
OUR SINS AND TO
CLEANSE US FROM ALL
UNRIGHTEOUSNESS.*

1 JOHN 1:9

KNOWING GOD THROUGH LOVE

1 John 4:1–19; Psalm 36; John 15:18–21; 1 Peter 2:1–3

1 John 4:1–19

THE SPIRIT OF TRUTH AND THE SPIRIT OF ERROR

¹ Dear friends, do not believe every spirit, but test the spirits to see if they are from God, because many false prophets have gone out into the world.

² This is how you know the Spirit of God: Every spirit that confesses that Jesus Christ has come in the flesh is from God, ³ but every spirit that does not confess Jesus is not from God. This is the spirit of the antichrist, which you have heard is coming; even now it is already in the world.

⁴ You are from God, little children, and you have conquered them, because the one who is in you is greater than the one who is in the world. ⁵ They are from the world. Therefore what they say is from the world, and the world listens to them. ⁶ We are from God. Anyone who knows God listens to us; anyone who is not from God does not listen to us. This is how we know the Spirit of truth and the spirit of deception.

KNOWING GOD THROUGH LOVE

⁷ Dear friends, let us love one another, because love is from God, and everyone who loves has been born of God and knows God. ⁸ The one who does not love

"For God loved the world in this way: He gave his one and only Son, so that everyone who believes in him will not perish but have eternal life."

JN 3:16

does not know God, because God is love. [9] God's love was revealed among us in this way: God sent his one and only Son into the world so that we might live through him. [10] Love consists in this: not that we loved God, but that he loved us and sent his Son to be the atoning sacrifice for our sins. [11] Dear friends, if God loved us in this way, we also must love one another. [12] No one has ever seen God. If we love one another, God remains in us and his love is made complete in us. [13] This is how we know that we remain in him and he in us: He has given us of his Spirit. [14] And we have seen and we testify that the Father has sent his Son as the world's Savior. [15] Whoever confesses that Jesus is the Son of God—God remains in him and he in God. [16] And we have come to know and to believe the love that God has for us.

God is love, and the one who remains in love remains in God, and God remains in him. [17] In this, love is made complete with us so that we may have confidence in the day of judgment, because as he is, so also are we in this world. [18] There is no fear in love; instead, perfect love drives out fear, because fear involves punishment. So the one who fears is not complete in love. [19] We love because he first loved us.

Psalm 36

HUMAN WICKEDNESS AND GOD'S LOVE

For the choir director. Of David, the LORD's servant.

[1] An oracle within my heart
concerning the transgression of the wicked person:
Dread of God has no effect on him.
[2] For with his flattering opinion of himself,
he does not discover and hate his iniquity.
[3] The words from his mouth are malicious and deceptive;
he has stopped acting wisely and doing good.
[4] Even on his bed he makes malicious plans.
He sets himself on a path that is not good,
and he does not reject evil.

[5] LORD, your faithful love reaches to heaven,
your faithfulness to the clouds.
[6] Your righteousness is like the highest mountains,
your judgments like the deepest sea.
LORD, you preserve people and animals.
[7] How priceless your faithful love is, God!
People take refuge in the shadow of your wings.

8 They are filled from the abundance of your house.
You let them drink from your refreshing stream.
9 For the wellspring of life is with you.
By means of your light we see light.

10 Spread your faithful love over those who know you,
and your righteousness over the upright in heart.
11 Do not let the foot of the arrogant come near me
or the hand of the wicked drive me away.
12 There! The evildoers have fallen.
They have been thrown down and cannot rise.

John 15:18–21

PERSECUTIONS PREDICTED

18 "If the world hates you, understand that it hated me before it hated you. 19 If you were of the world, the world would love you as its own. However, because you are not of the world, but I have chosen you out of it, the world hates you. 20 Remember the word I spoke to you: 'A servant is not greater than his master.' If they persecuted me, they will also persecute you. If they kept my word, they will also keep yours. 21 But they will do all these things to you on account of my name, because they don't know the one who sent me."

1 Peter 2:1–3

THE LIVING STONE AND A HOLY PEOPLE

1 Therefore, rid yourselves of all malice, all deceit, hypocrisy, envy, and all slander. 2 Like newborn infants, desire the pure milk of the word, so that you may grow up into your salvation, 3 if you have tasted that the Lord is good.

USE THIS VERSE FROM
YOUR DAILY READING AS
A PROMPT FOR PRAYER.

*Dear friends, let us love one another,
because love is from God, and everyone
who loves has been born of God and
knows God.*

1 JOHN 4:7

LOVE
IN THE BIBLE

Christlike love is central to the gospel. This theme is especially prominent in 1 John, which describes how loving God and loving others is key to becoming more like Jesus. There are many words in Hebrew and Greek that are translated "love" in our English Bibles, but each has its own special emphasis. On the following page are a few of the most common biblical words for love, along with their descriptions and some key places they appear in Scripture.

AHEB

aw-habe'
HEBREW: to love, care for

Aheb is the most common Hebrew word translated as "love" in the Old Testament. It has a wide range of meaning, including the love a parent has for a child, the romantic feelings a man has for a woman, affection for a friend, and the human appetite for food and sleep.

GENESIS 22:2
GENESIS 29:20
DEUTERONOMY 7:8–9
2 SAMUEL 1:26

CHESED

kheh'-sed
HEBREW: goodness, kindness

In the Old Testament, *chesed* almost always describes God's faithful lovingkindness to His people within the context of a covenant.

EXODUS 15:13
NUMBERS 14:19
DEUTERONOMY 5:9–10
PSALM 136

AGAPAO

ag-ap-ah'-o
GREEK: to love, esteem

In the New Testament, *agapao* refers to a kind of love that expresses personal will and affection. In some instances, it includes an aspect of duty or submission. It describes God's love for believers and the Father's love for the Son. With one exception (3 John 9), John uses *agapao* excusively in these three letters.

MATTHEW 6:24
JOHN 13:34
1 JOHN 4:7–21

PHILEO

fil-eh'-o
GREEK: to love, kiss

In the New Testament, *phileo* often describes love or affection for a friend, but it can also refer to a love of things.

MATTHEW 10:37
MATTHEW 23:6
REVELATION 22:15

LOVING OUR BROTHERS & SISTERS

1 John 4:20–21; 1 John 5:1–13; Romans 13:8–14; 1 Corinthians 13

20 If anyone says, "I love God," and yet hates his brother or sister, he is a liar. For the person who does not love his brother or sister whom he has seen cannot love God whom he has not seen. 21 And we have this command from him: The one who loves God must also love his brother and sister.

1 Everyone who believes that Jesus is the Christ has been born of God, and everyone who loves the Father also loves the one born of him. 2 This is how we know that we love God's children: when we love God and obey his commands. 3 For this is what love for God is: to keep his commands. And his commands are not a burden, 4 because everyone who has been born of God conquers the world. This is the victory that has conquered the world: our faith.

THE CERTAINTY OF GOD'S TESTIMONY

> THE ONE WHO LOVES GOD MUST ALSO LOVE HIS BROTHER AND SISTER.
>
> 1 JOHN 4:21

5 Who is the one who conquers the world but the one who believes that Jesus is the Son of God? 6 Jesus Christ—he is the one who came by water and blood, not by water only, but by water and by blood. And the Spirit is the one who testifies, because the Spirit is the truth. 7 For there are three that testify: 8 the Spirit, the water, and the blood—and these three are in agreement. 9 If we accept human testimony, God's testimony is greater, because it is God's testimony that he has given about his Son. 10 The one who believes in the Son of God has this testimony within himself. The one who does not believe God has made him a liar, because he has not believed in the testimony God has given about his Son. 11 And this is the testimony: God has given us eternal life, and this life is in his Son. 12 The one who has the Son has life. The one who does not have the Son of God does not have life. 13 I have written these things to you who believe in the name of the Son of God so that you may know that you have eternal life.

LOVE, OUR PRIMARY DUTY

8 Do not owe anyone anything, except to love one another, for the one who loves another has fulfilled the law. 9 The commandments, Do not commit adultery; do not murder; do not steal; do not covet; and any other commandment, are summed up by this commandment: Love your neighbor as yourself. 10 Love does no wrong to a neighbor. Love, therefore, is the fulfillment of the law.

[11] Besides this, since you know the time, it is already the hour for youto wake up from sleep, because now our salvation is nearer than when we first believed. [12] The night is nearly over, and the day is near; so let us discard the deeds of darkness and put on the armor of light. [13] Let us walk with decency, as in the daytime: not in carousing and drunkenness; not in sexual impurity and promiscuity; not in quarreling and jealousy. [14] But put on the Lord Jesus Christ, and don't make plans to gratify the desires of the flesh.

1 Corinthians 13

LOVE: THE SUPERIOR WAY

[1] If I speak human or angelic tongues but do not have love, I am a noisy gong or a clanging cymbal. [2] If I have the gift of prophecy and understand all mysteries and all knowledge, and if I have all faith so that I can move mountains but do not have love, I am nothing. [3] And if I give away all my possessions, and if I give over my body in order to boast but do not have love, I gain nothing.

[4] Love is patient, love is kind. Love does not envy, is not boastful, is not arrogant, [5] is not rude, is not self-seeking, is not irritable, and does not keep a record of wrongs. [6] Love finds no joy in unrighteousness but rejoices in the truth. [7] It bears all things, believes all things, hopes all things, endures all things.

[8] Love never ends. But as for prophecies, they will come to an end; as for tongues, they will cease; as for knowledge, it will come to an end. [9] For we know in part, and we prophesy in part, [10] but when the perfect comes, the partial will come to an end. [11] When I was a child, I spoke like a child, I thought like a child, I reasoned like a child. When I became a man, I put aside childish things. [12] For now we see only a reflection as in a mirror, but then face to face. Now I know in part, but then I will know fully, as I am fully known. [13] Now these three remain: faith, hope, and love—but the greatest of these is love.

*For the person who does not love his
brother or sister whom he has seen
cannot love God whom he has not seen.*

1 JOHN 4:20

SHOULD I LOVE MY BROTHER OR SISTER IN CHRIST?

Common Objections Answered in 1 John

5
WHAT IF I AM AFRAID?

There is no fear in love; instead, perfect love drives out fear…

1JN 4:18

1
WHY SHOULD I LOVE THIS PERSON?

Dear friends, if God loved us in this way, we also must love one another.

1JN 4:11

4
DOES IT REALLY MATTER IF I LOVE THIS PERSON?

The one who loves his brother or sister remains in the light, and there is no cause for stumbling in him.

1JN 2:10

2
WHAT IF THEY DON'T LOVE ME?

We love because he first loved us.

1JN 4:19

3
WHAT IF I DON'T LIKE THEM?

If anyone says, "I love God," and yet hates his brother or sister, he is a liar. For the person who does not love his brother or sister whom he has seen cannot love God whom he has not seen.

1JN 4:20

6 DOES GOD REALLY CARE IF I LOVE THIS PERSON?

And we have this command from him: The one who loves God must also love his brother and sister.

1JN 4:21

7 HOW MUCH MUST I LOVE?

This is how we have come to know love: He laid down his life for us. We should also lay down our lives for our brothers and sisters.

1JN 3:16

8 WHAT DOES LOVE LOOK LIKE?

Little children, let us not love in word or speech, but in action and in truth.

1JN 3:18

10 HOW WILL I KNOW WHEN I TRULY LOVE THIS PERSON?

This is how we know that we love God's children: when we love God and obey his commands.

1JN 5:2

9 WHAT IS AT STAKE IF I DON'T LOVE THIS PERSON?

This is how God's children and the devil's children become obvious. Whoever does not do what is right is not of God, especially the one who does not love his brother or sister.

1JN 3:10

We know that we have passed from death to life because we love our brothers and sisters. The one who does not love remains in death.

1JN 3:14

If anyone has this world's goods and sees a fellow believer in need but withholds compassion from him—how does God's love reside in him?

1JN 3:17

EFFECTIVE PRAYER

1 John 5:14–21; Deuteronomy 29:29; Luke 18:1–8; John 3:16–17

EFFECTIVE PRAYER

[14] This is the confidence we have before him: If we ask anything according to his will, he hears us. [15] And if we know that he hears whatever we ask, we know that we have what we have asked of him.

[16] If anyone sees a fellow believer committing a sin that doesn't lead to death, he should ask, and God will give life to him—to those who commit sin that doesn't lead to death. There is sin that leads to death. I am not saying he should pray about that. [17] All unrighteousness is sin, and there is sin that doesn't lead to death.

CONCLUSION

IF WE ASK ANYTHING ACCORDING TO HIS WILL, HE HEARS US.

1 JOHN 5:14

[18] We know that everyone who has been born of God does not sin, but the one who is born of God keeps him, and the evil one does not touch him. [19] We know that we are of God, and the whole world is under the sway of the evil one. [20] And we know that the Son of God has come and has given us understanding so that we may know the true one. We are in the true one—that is, in his Son Jesus Christ. He is the true God and eternal life.

[21] Little children, guard yourselves from idols.

The hidden things belong to the LORD our God, but the revealed things belong to us and our children forever, so that we may follow all the words of this law.

THE PARABLE OF THE PERSISTENT WIDOW

[1] Now he told them a parable on the need for them to pray always and not give up. [2] "There was a judge in a certain town who didn't fear God or respect people. [3] And a widow in that town kept coming to him, saying, 'Give me justice against my adversary.'

[4] "For a while he was unwilling, but later he said to himself, 'Even though I don't fear God or respect people, [5] yet because this widow keeps pestering me, I will give her justice, so that she doesn't wear me out by her persistent coming.'"

6 Then the Lord said, "Listen to what the unjust judge says. 7 Will not God grant justice to his elect who cry out to him day and night? Will he delay helping them? 8 I tell you that he will swiftly grant them justice. Nevertheless, when the Son of Man comes, will he find faith on earth?"

John 3:16–17

16 For God loved the world in this way: He gave his one and only Son, so that everyone who believes in him will not perish but have eternal life. 17 For God did not send his Son into the world to condemn the world, but to save the world through him.

*And if we know that he hears
whatever we ask, we know that we
have what we have asked of him.*

1 JOHN 5:15

*THIS IS LOVE: THAT
WE WALK ACCORDING
TO HIS COMMANDS.
THIS IS THE COMMAND
AS YOU HAVE
HEARD IT FROM THE
BEGINNING: THAT YOU
WALK IN LOVE.*

Message & Purpose

Like Jesus, who wept over Jerusalem (Lk 19:41), and Paul, who wrote of "the daily pressure" of his "concern for all the churches" (2Co 11:28), John was concerned about his congregation. Would they neglect to embody God's love for one another? Would they fall prey to false teachers? Second John was written with pastoral love and concern for the fledgling church.

John's message is clear: walk in the truth, obey God's commandments, love one another, and guard the teachings of Christ. John also confirmed the spiritual safety of the believing community with a beginning and ending reference to their election by God (2Jn 1, 13).

Give Thanks for the Book of 2 John

It is easy for congregations to get off track. John encourages believers to stay the course by responding to one another with love, exhorting them to partner this love with the truth of the gospel. Second John heartens believers for steadfastness in Christ and hope to "receive a full reward" (v. 8).

WALKING IN LOVE

2 John; John 8:31–32; 1 Corinthians 3:6–9

2 John

GREETING

¹ The elder:

To the elect lady and her children, whom I love in the truth—and not only I, but also all who know the truth— ² because of the truth that remains in us and will be with us forever.

³ Grace, mercy, and peace will be with us from God the Father and from Jesus Christ, the Son of the Father, in truth and love.

TRUTH AND DECEPTION

GOSPEL CONNECTION

"I give you a new command: Love one another. Just as I have loved you, you are also to love one another."
JN 13:34

⁴ I was very glad to find some of your children walking in truth, in keeping with a command we have received from the Father. ⁵ So now I ask you, dear lady—not as if I were writing you a new command, but one we have had from the beginning—that we love one another. ⁶ This is love: that we walk according to his commands. This is the command as you have heard it from the beginning: that you walk in love.

⁷ Many deceivers have gone out into the world; they do not confess the coming of Jesus Christ in the flesh. This is the deceiver and the antichrist. ⁸ Watch yourselves so you don't lose what we have worked for, but that you may receive a full reward. ⁹ Anyone who does not remain in Christ's teaching but goes beyond it does not have God. The one who remains in that teaching, this one has both the Father and the Son. ¹⁰ If anyone comes to you and does not bring this teaching, do not receive him into your home, and don't greet him; ¹¹ for the one who greets him shares in his evil works.

FAREWELL

GOSPEL CONNECTION

"I have told you these things so that my joy may be in you and your joy may be complete."
JN 15:11

¹² Though I have many things to write to you, I don't want to use paper and ink. Instead, I hope to come to you and talk face to face so that our joy may be complete.

¹³ The children of your elect sister send you greetings.

John 8:31–32

31 Then Jesus said to the Jews who had believed him, "If you continue in my word, you really are my disciples. 32 You will know the truth, and the truth will set you free."

1 Corinthians 3:6–9

6 I planted, Apollos watered, but God gave the growth. 7 So then neither the one who plants nor the one who waters is anything, but only God who gives the growth. 8 Now he who plants and he who waters are one, and each will receive his own reward according to his own labor. 9 For we are God's coworkers. You are God's field, God's building.

*This is love: that we walk according to
his commands. This is the command as
you have heard it from the beginning:
that you walk in love.*

2 JOHN 6

---

*I HAVE NO GREATER
JOY THAN THIS:
TO HEAR THAT
MY CHILDREN ARE
WALKING IN TRUTH.*

A Little Background

Second and 3 John are often described as "twin epistles." There are some significant similarities between the two letters that are worth noting.

In both epistles:

1. The author described himself as "the elder" (2Jn 1; 3Jn 1).

2. The recipients were those whom he loved "in the truth" (2Jn 1; 3Jn 1).

3. The recipients were a cause for great gladness by John (2Jn 4; 3Jn 3).

4. The recipients were "walking in the truth" (2Jn 4; 3Jn 3), and the elder had received good reports about them (2Jn 4; 3Jn 3–4).

5. The letters contain a warning (2Jn 8; 3Jn 9–11).

6. The elder desired to see the recipients face to face (2Jn 12; 3Jn 14).

7. The elder delivered greetings from others (2Jn 13; 3Jn 14).

Message & Purpose

Third John is a personal letter that revolves around three individuals: Gaius, the recipient of the letter; Diotrephes, the one causing trouble; and Demetrius, who was probably the bearer of the letter. The purpose was to give a word of exhortation to Gaius and encourage him not to imitate the bad example of Diotrephes. Instead, Gaius was to continue the good work he was doing in receiving and supporting the traveling teachers or missionaries.

Give Thanks for the Book of 3 John

This brief letter underscores central Christian convictions and testifies to the God-centeredness of the Christian faith (3Jn 7, 11). Jesus and the Spirit are not mentioned specifically (unless "the truth itself" in 3 John 12 refers to Jesus; see Jn 14:6; 1Jn 5:20). But in the writer's view, Jesus and the Spirit were undoubtedly included in the reference to "God," whose "truth" this letter appeals to so frequently (3Jn 1, 3–4, 8, 12).

IMITATING WHAT IS GOOD

3 John; Matthew 20:25–28; Hebrews 13:1–6

3 John

GREETING

[1] The elder:

To my dear friend Gaius, whom I love in the truth.

GOSPEL CONNECTION

"You are a king then?" Pilate asked.

"You say that I'm a king," Jesus replied. "I was born for this, and I have come into the world for this: to testify to the truth. Everyone who is of the truth listens to my voice."

JN 18:37

[2] Dear friend, I pray that you are prospering in every way and are in good health, just as your whole life is going well. [3] For I was very glad when fellow believers came and testified to your fidelity to the truth—how you are walking in truth. [4] I have no greater joy than this: to hear that my children are walking in truth.

GAIUS COMMENDED

[5] Dear friend, you are acting faithfully in whatever you do for the brothers and sisters, especially when they are strangers. [6] They have testified to your love before the church. You will do well to send them on their journey in a manner worthy of God, [7] since they set out for the sake of the Name, accepting nothing from pagans. [8] Therefore, we ought to support such people so that we can be coworkers with the truth.

DIOTREPHES AND DEMETRIUS

[9] I wrote something to the church, but Diotrephes, who loves to have first place among them, does not receive our authority. [10] This is why, if I come, I will remind him of the works he is doing, slandering us with malicious words. And he is not satisfied with that! He not only refuses to welcome fellow believers, but he even stops those who want to do so and expels them from the church.

[11] Dear friend, do not imitate what is evil, but what is good. The one who does good is of God; the one who does evil has not seen God. [12] Everyone speaks well of Demetrius—even the truth itself. And we also speak well of him, and you know that our testimony is true.

FAREWELL

[13] I have many things to write you, but I don't want to write to you with pen and ink. [14] I hope to see you soon, and we will talk face to face.

[15] Peace to you. The friends send you greetings. Greet the friends by name.

Matthew 20:25–28

[25] Jesus called them over and said, "You know that the rulers of the Gentiles lord it over them, and those in high positions act as tyrants over them. [26] It must not be like that among you. On the contrary, whoever wants to become great among you must be your servant, [27] and whoever wants to be first among you must be your slave; [28] just as the Son of Man did not come to be served, but to serve, and to give his life as a ransom for many."

Hebrews 13:1–6

FINAL EXHORTATIONS

[1] Let brotherly love continue. [2] Don't neglect to show hospitality, for by doing this some have welcomed angels as guests without knowing it. [3] Remember those in prison, as though you were in prison with them, and the mistreated, as though you yourselves were suffering bodily. [4] Marriage is to be honored by all and the marriage bed kept undefiled, because God will judge the sexually immoral and adulterers. [5] Keep your life free from the love of money. Be satisfied with what you have, for he himself has said, I will never leave you or abandon you. [6] Therefore, we may boldly say,

The Lord is my helper;
I will not be afraid.
What can man do to me?

USE THIS VERSE FROM
YOUR DAILY READING AS
A PROMPT FOR PRAYER.

*The one who does good is of God; the
one who does evil has not seen God.*

3 JOHN 11

ASSURANCES OF THE GOSPEL

While the letters themselves don't tell us the precise nature of the false teaching John wrote to combat, many Bible commentators believe it was an early form of gnosticism—a heresy claiming that special, or secret, knowledge was the path to salvation. To refute this false teaching, John highlighted what the recipients of his letters already knew as followers of Christ.

John's pastoral letters are filled with words of confidence. Below are twenty-five of them.

1JN 1:1–3

They know they have fellowship with the Father, the Son, and the community of believers.

1JN 2:1

They know Christ is their advocate in the face of sin.

1JN 2:3

They know they have come to Christ because they keep His commands.

1JN 2:8

They know darkness is passing and light is coming.

1JN 2:12–14

They know Christ and the Father, who are eternal.

1JN 2:17

They know that while the world is passing away, the one who does God's will remains forever.

1JN 2:20–21

They know the truth because they have the Holy Spirit.

1JN 2:27

They know the Holy Spirit lives in them and teaches them.

1JN 2:29

They know their righteousness is found in Christ.

1JN 3:2

They know that when Christ appears, they will be like Him.

1JN 3:14

They know they have passed from death unto life.

1JN 3:16

They know the love of Christ because He laid down His life for them.

1JN 3:19–20

They know they are in the truth, and their own hearts can't condemn them.

1JN 3:24

They know they are joined to God by the Holy Spirit who lives in them.

1JN 4:2

They know the Spirit confesses: Jesus has come in the flesh.

1JN 4:4

They know the One who is in them is greater than he who is in the world.

1JN 4:9–10

They know Christ made payment for their sins.

1JN 4:13–15

They know the Father sent His Son to be the Savior of the world and His Holy Spirit to dwell in them.

1JN 5:1–5

They know that by faith they have been born of God, and they know they have overcome the world.

1JN 5:11–12

They know that whoever has the Son has life.

1JN 5:13–15

They know they have eternal life, and that God will hear anything they ask of Him, and answer according to His perfect will.

1JN 5:20

They know that the Son of God gives understanding.

2JN 6

They know that His commands are constant.

2JN 9

They know that whoever abides in the teachings of Christ has both the Father and the Son.

3JN 12

They know John's testimony is true.

DAY THIRTEEN

GRACE DAY

Use today to pray, rest, and reflect on this week's reading, giving thanks for the grace that is ours in Christ.

WE LOVE BECAUSE HE FIRST LOVED US.

1 JOHN 4:19

14

WEEKLY TRUTH

Scripture is God-breathed and true. When we memorize it, we carry the gospel with us wherever we go.

This week we will memorize the key verse for 2 John, a description of what it looks like to love God.

THIS IS LOVE:
THAT WE WALK
ACCORDING TO HIS
COMMANDS.

2 JOHN 6a

_____

*"IF WE HAVE GOT
THE TRUE LOVE OF
GOD SHED ABROAD
IN OUR HEARTS, WE
WILL SHOW IT IN OUR
LIFE. WE WILL NOT
HAVE TO GO UP AND
DOWN THE EARTH
PROCLAIMING IT; WE
WILL SHOW IT IN
EVERYTHING WE SAY
OR DO."*

_____

DOWNLOAD THE APP

VISIT
shereadstruth.com

SHOP
shopshereadstruth.com

CONTACT
hello@shereadstruth.com

CONNECT
@shereadstruth
#shereadstruth

LISTEN
She Reads Truth Podcast

BIBLIOGRAPHY

Freedman, David Noel, ed. *Eerdmans Dictionary of the Bible*. Grand Rapids, MI: Wm. B. Eerdmans
    Publishing Co., 2000.

"Love." In *Lexham Theological Wordbook*, Mangum, Douglas, Derek R. Brown, and Rachel Klippenstein.
    Bellingham, WA: Lexham Press., 2014.

"Love." In *The Lexham Bible Dictionary*, Barry, John D., David Bomar, Derek R. Brown, Douglas Mangum,
    Elliot Ritzema, Lazarus Wentz, Wendy Widder, Carrie Sinclair Wolcott. Bellingham, WA: Lexham
    Press. 2016.

BE A WOMAN IN THE WORD OF GOD EVERY DAY

Reading the Bible every day can feel like a challenge, but She Reads Truth is here to help each step of the way. When you sign up for the She Reads Truth Subscription Box, you will get Truth delivered right to your doorstep, for just $20 a month.

SHE READS TRUTH SUBSCRIPTION BOX BENEFITS

- Each new, beautifully designed Study Book—at least one per month

- Free access to our complete database of 75+ plans on the She Reads Truth App

- Exclusive merch and giveaways throughout the year

- Early access to online sales

- Flexible delivery options for your monthly shipment

SHOPSHEREADSTRUTH.COM/BOX

FOR THE RECORD

WHERE DID I STUDY?

O HOME
O OFFICE
O COFFEE SHOP
O CHURCH
O A FRIEND'S HOUSE
O OTHER

WHAT WAS I LISTENING TO?

ARTIST:

SONG:

PLAYLIST:

WHEN DID I STUDY?

MORNING

AFTERNOON

NIGHT

What did I learn?

WHAT WAS HAPPENING IN MY LIFE?

WHAT WAS HAPPENING IN THE WORLD?

MONTH	DAY	YEAR

END DATE

IF WE CONFESS OUR
SINS, HE IS FAITHFUL
AND RIGHTEOUS
TO FORGIVE US
OUR SINS AND TO
CLEANSE US FROM ALL
UNRIGHTEOUSNESS.

1 JOHN 1:9

LET'S MEMORIZE
GOD'S WORD TOGETHER.

These Scripture memory cards
correspond to the Weekly Truths in
the **1, 2 & 3 John** reading plan.

Punch out the cards and carry them
with you, place them where you'll
see them often, or share them with
a friend.

THIS IS LOVE: THAT WE
WALK ACCORDING TO
HIS COMMANDS.

2 JOHN 6a

I HAVE NO
GREATER JOY
THAN THIS: TO
HEAR THAT MY
CHILDREN ARE
WALKING IN
TRUTH.

3 JOHN 4

Bonus Card

SHE READS TRUTH

WOMEN IN THE WORD
OF GOD EVERY DAY

SHEREADSTRUTH.COM
hello@shereadstruth.com
@shereadstruth

SHE READS TRUTH

WOMEN IN THE WORD
OF GOD EVERY DAY

SHEREADSTRUTH.COM
hello@shereadstruth.com
@shereadstruth

SHE READS TRUTH

WOMEN IN THE WORD
OF GOD EVERY DAY

SHEREADSTRUTH.COM
hello@shereadstruth.com
@shereadstruth